SNARKY SHARK

THIS EDITION

Editorial Management by Oriel Square
Produced for DK by WonderLab Group LLC
Jennifer Emmett, Erica Green, Kate Hale, *Founders*

Editor Maya Myers; **Photography Editor** Nicole DiMella; **Managing Editor** Rachel Houghton;
Designers Project Design Company; **Researcher** Michelle Harris;
Copy Editor Lori Merritt; **Indexer** Connie Binder; **Proofreader** Susan K. Hom;
Sensitivity Reader Ebonye Gussine Wilkins; **Series Reading Specialist** Dr. Jennifer Albro

First American Edition, 2024
Published in the United States by DK Publishing, a division of Penguin Random House LLC
1745 Broadway, 20th Floor, New York, NY 10019

Text and Illustration Copyright © Wonderlab Group, LLC 2024
24 25 26 27 10 9 8 7 6 5 4 3 2 1
001-342890-Oct/2024

A catalog record for this book is available from the Library of Congress.
HC ISBN: 978-0-5938-4723-7
PB ISBN: 978-0-5938-4722-0

DK books are available at special discounts when purchased in bulk for sales promotions, premiums, fund-raising, or educational use. For details, contact:
DK Publishing Special Markets, 1745 Broadway, 20th Floor, New York, NY 10019
SpecialSales@dk.com

Printed and bound in China

The publisher would like to thank the following for their kind permission to reproduce their images: a=above; c=center; b=below; l=left; r=right; t=top; b/g=background
vendor: 123RF.com: ladadikart 17br, 26bc, 32bc; **Alamy Stock Photo:** AJ Pics / © DISNEY 24clb, All Star Picture Library / UNIVERSAL 25tr, BIOSPHOTO / Jeffrey Rotman 12tl, Blue Planet Archive JMI 13cla, Corbin17 23, Paul Glaser / dpa 24crb, Maximum Film / © SYFY 25clb, Louise Murray 9tl, Natural History Museum, London 22br, © Universal Pictures / Courtesy Everett Collection 25cla, WaterFrame_fba 18t, Poelzer Wolfgang 10crb (Cat shark); **Ardea:** Paulo Di Oliviera 9cra; **Dorling Kindersley:** Gaz Weisman - Wonderlab 24cra, 28br, 29tr, Wonderlab - Gaz Weisman 9br; **Dreamstime.com:** Noviantoko Tri Arijanto 8b, Artisticco Llc 1b, 3clb, Yann Hubert 18cb, Juladyphoto 28bl, Lukaves 21, Marcos Calvo Mesa 11tc, Sean Steininger 19cb, Whitepointer 3cb; **Getty Images:** Collection Mix: Subjects / Caia Image 29t, Pedro Mera / Stringer 24bl, Moment / Allan Davey 16-17b, Publisher Mix / Cultura 26-27, RooM / torstenvelden 10bl, Todd Winner / Stocktrek Images 4-5; **Getty Images / iStock:** atese 1cb, Eivaisla 24-25, kenzaza 12-13, Mark Kostich 17tr, LadadikArt 23bl, 25bc, 30b, Nigel Marsh 14-15, NatalyaBurova 3crb (bl), 10cb (x3), 12cra, 14bl, 15br, Nerthuz 12cr, paulbcowell 13br, Philip Thurston 10-11; **naturepl.com:** Juergen Freund 19cla, Andy Murch 11cra, Doug Perrine 6-7; **Science Photo Library:** Richard Bizley 20b; **Shutterstock.com:** frantisekhojdysz 8cb, Tomas Kotouc 11crb, oneinchpunch 25cr

Cover images: *Front:* **Getty Images:** Moment / by wildestanimal; **Getty Images / iStock:** clairevis ca/ (clown fish); *Back:* **Getty Images / iStock:** maxbod cra

All other images © Dorling Kindersley Limited
For more information see: www.dkimages.com

www.dk.com

MIX
Paper | Supporting responsible forestry
FSC™ C018179

This book was made with Forest Stewardship Council™ certified paper – one small step in DK's commitment to a sustainable future.
Learn more at **www.dk.com/uk/information/sustainability**

Level
2

SNARKY SHARKS

Becky Baines

DK

Contents

Howdy!

Ruler of the Ocean

What's fierce and finned and has more fans than most movie stars? Sharks! How much do you know about the most famous fish in the sea?

I was really craving some cafeteria fish sticks.

Some sharks swim alone. Some swim in pairs. A group of sharks that live together can be called a school or a shiver.

Sharks live in oceans all over the world.

Many sharks swim near sunny coral reefs and beaches where there are lots of smaller fish to eat. But some of these ocean oddballs live in surprising places!

Caribbean reef shark

Greenland shark

Boo!

goblin
shark

In the deepest part of the ocean, spooky goblin sharks have special skills to help them hunt in the dark.

Under the Arctic ice, Greenland sharks move super slow through the freezing water.

Bull sharks can even live in rivers!

Give me a tropical beach any day!

9

We Are Family

Did you know there are around 500 different kinds of sharks?

Some are as small as a goldfish. Others can grow bigger than a whale! Many are gray, but others are brown, black, or even pink. Some types of sharks have speckles, spots, and stripes.

Wait, I have fins back there?

But as different as they may look, they all have those telltale fins!

Sharks have four types of fins (or even five). The most famous fin is the dorsal fin— that's the big one that sticks up out of the water when sharks swim near the surface. Most sharks have a smaller dorsal fin, too. The dorsal fins help keep their heavy bodies upright so they don't roll over.

11

Some sharks have amazing body parts.

How'd you do on the oceanography test?

megamouth shark

Nailed it!

hammerhead shark

Hammerheads have long heads shaped like rectangles, with eyes on either side. This helps them see all around them all the time.

Megamouth sharks have huge mouths and teeny-tiny teeth. Scientists believe they take big gulps of water and swish it through their teeth. They find tiny creatures called plankton to eat.

 **cookiecutter shark**

Cookiecutter sharks are tiny but mighty. They can take a bite out of a bigger fish like a cookie cutter cuts out dough.

The whale shark is a gentle giant. This school bus–sized shark is the biggest fish in the whole sea!

whale shark

What Big Teeth You Have!

Most sharks are predators. They hunt fish and seals to eat. Their teeth are their tools to catch, crunch, and sift.

Sharp, pointy teeth are sharks' claim to fame. There are actually four different kinds of shark teeth!

Sand tiger sharks have super-sharp teeth like needles.
The pointy ends are good for catching smaller, faster meals.

I'll take one large Snappy Meal to go!

sand tiger shark

Great white sharks have teeth shaped like triangles. They are perfect for digging into big fish. They have edges like knives to help rip up their food. But great whites don't use their teeth to chew! They swallow their food in chunks.

Word of Mouth

Great white sharks have lots of rows of sharp, pointy teeth. They fall out and grow back over and over again. Some sharks can go through 30,000 teeth in their lives! If you're lucky, you might find shark teeth on a beach.

The tooth fairy owes me big time!

nurse shark feeding on lionfish

Burp!

Nurse sharks have flat teeth. They are made for crunching through the shells of crabs and snails.

The biggest sharks have teeth that don't work like teeth at all! Whale sharks use their teeth as a screen to sift tiny shrimp and plankton out of the water.

whale shark teeth

I was voted "Best Smile" in my whole school.

whale shark

Meet the Meg

If you think a great white is massive, be glad you can never meet a megalodon! About 2.5 million years ago, megalodon sharks ruled the sea.

Back then, many animals on Earth grew much bigger than they do today. The megalodon was the top predator. Scientists think it may have been as long as three great whites and heavier than a sperm whale! It ate large fish, whales, and even other sharks.

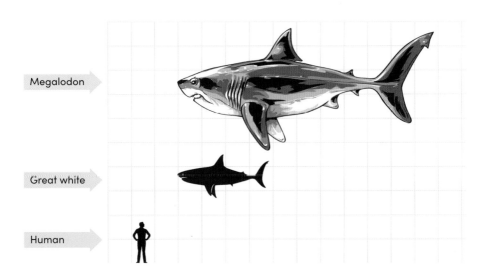

Megalodon

Great white

Human

The megalodon isn't here to tell us about itself, so scientists look for clues. Like sharks today, megalodon sharks left behind teeth that can tell us a lot about their lives. From the size and shape of its teeth, we can use what we know about great whites to tell us how big the megalodon was, and what it ate.

Scientists have also found megalodon fossils that help us understand its size.

A Blast from the Past

Fossils are remains from animals that lived a long time ago. People have found fossils of entire dinosaur skeletons! But so far, they have only found the teeth and backbone of a megalodon.

Famous Fish Faces

There's a reason sharks are the celebrities of the sea. See how many of these famous fish you know.

Funny story, I actually turned down that role ...

Bruce

Brooklyn

Megalodon

Vroom!

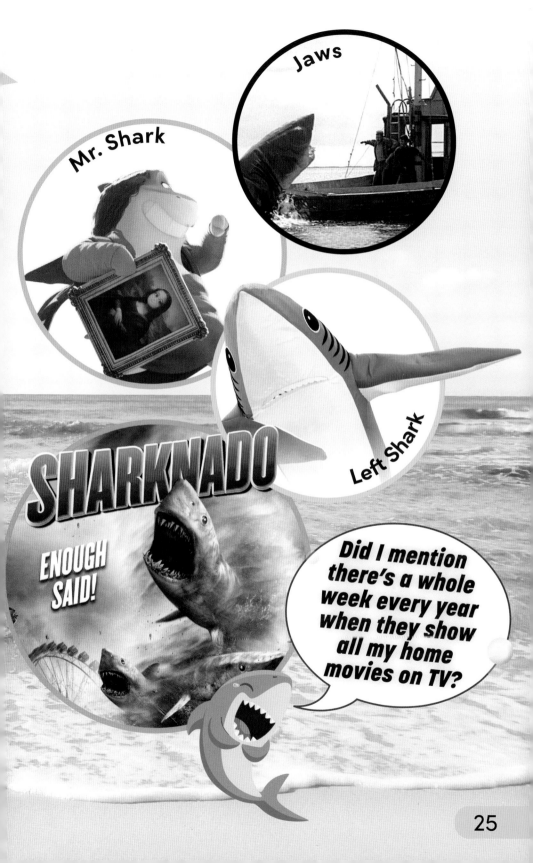

To the Rescue!

It may sound strange that a predator as tough as a shark could need our help. But like many ocean animals, sharks are in trouble.

Some humans hunt sharks for food, or sometimes just for their fins. Many sharks have live babies, instead of laying lots of eggs like other fish.

Don't take the bait!

That means they don't reproduce as quickly. Because of this, some sharks are being killed faster than they are being replaced. This is called overfishing.

Humans don't just hurt the sharks; they also hurt sharks' homes. When we visit the ocean, we don't always think about the animals that live there. We can be careless with things like plastic and chemicals. These harm coral reefs. When reefs no longer make good homes, fish stay away. That makes it hard for sharks to find food.

You don't see me coming to your house and leaving my trash everywhere.

Did Somebody Say Shark Hero?

When you are out in nature, remember: you're visiting an animal's natural habitat, or home! At the beach, take your trash with you when you leave. If you see someone else's trash left behind, pick it up and throw it away if it's safe to do so. And if you collect shells, make sure no animals are living in them!

I'd help you out, but I don't have thumbs!

You can help sharks by learning everything you can and talking with your friends about sharks. Caring about animals is the first step to helping them!

Glossary

Cartilage
Firm but flexible tissue in the body

Coral reef
A group of living coral that clumps together and acts as living space for many ocean animals

Dorsal fin
The large fin on the back of many ocean animals

Fossils
The remains or traces of animal life that existed a long time ago

Habitat
A place where things naturally live and grow

Megalodon
An enormous shark that lived on Earth 2.5 million years ago

Overfishing
Taking fish from the ocean faster than they can reproduce

Plastic
A manmade material that takes a very long time to break down in nature

Predator
An animal that hunts and eats other animals

Reproduce
To have babies

School
A group of animals, usually fish

Index

Quiz

Answer the questions to see what you have learned. Check your answers in the key below.

1. What does a megamouth shark eat?

2. How many teeth can a great white shark grow and replace in its lifetime?

3. Which shark has a wide, rectangle-shaped head?

4. How do scientists know how big the megalodon was?

5. What is it called when fish are killed faster than they reproduce?

1. Plankton 2. 30,000 3. Hammerhead 4. Teeth and fossils
5. Overfishing